PEEL

MERVYN MORRIS (b. 1937 in Kingston, Jamaica) studied at the University College of the West Indies and, as a Rhodes Scholar, at St Edmund Hall, Oxford. He taught at the University of the West Indies, retiring in 2002 as Professor of Creative Writing and West Indian Literature.

He is the author of *'Is English We Speaking' and Other Essays* (1999), *Making West Indian Literature* (2005) and *Miss Lou: Louise Bennett and Jamaican Culture* (2014). His collections of poetry are *The Pond* (1973, revised 1997), *Shadowboxing* (1979), *Examination Centre* (1992), *Vestiges* (a limited edition, 1996), *On Holy Week* (1976, 1993, 2016), and *I been there, sort of: New and Selected Poems* (2006). A Poetry Archive recording of him reading became available in 2011. He received Jamaica's Order of Merit in 2009, and was appointed Poet Laureate in 2014.

Also by Mervyn Morris

POETRY
The Pond
Shadowboxing
Examination Centre
Vestiges
On Holy Week
I been there, sort of

CRITICISM & BIOGRAPHY
'Is English We Speaking' and Other Essays
Making West Indian Literature
Miss Lou: Louise Bennett and Jamaican Culture

Peelin Orange

the colleѐted poems of

MERVYN
MORRIS

CARCANET

First published in Great Britain in 2017 by
Carcanet Press Limited
Alliance House, 30 Cross Street,
Manchester, M2 7AQ
www.carcanet.co.uk

A CIP catalogue record for this book is available from
the British Library, ISBN 9781784104580

The publisher acknowledges financial
assistance from Arts Council England.

Supported using public funding by
ARTS COUNCIL
ENGLAND

for Helen

CONTENTS

I DRAW NEAR

II   LOVE IS

III   ON HOLY WEEK

I DRAW NEAR

WALK GOOD

Teck time
walk good

Yu buck yu foot
an memory ketch yu

like a springe

A DRAWING

after M.C. Escher

the vaulted building
overlooks the sea

grave faces locked
in iron devotion
two files of monks
go ritually up and down
those stairs

one gawping solitary
brother down below
is wondering why
the cowled monks
keep on walking walking

below him still
another one is
turned away
from all that
self-abusing he

is looking down
to sea

THE MUSIC ROOM

to you
who come to hear confession
in the music room

we seem
to know the score
by art

embroidering
the flash
of revelation

hush now, something's coming
in a rush of silence
in the too much light
something's coming, hush

AT A POETRY READING

Negotiating strangers
and inscrutable desires,
the old pretenders hope to be
accepted as constructive liars.

If, playing parts, they can avoid the spurious
(the false pretence, the histrionic fraud)
and manage the occasional epiphany,
some of the other actors will applaud.

PEELIN ORANGE

Dem use to seh
yu peel a orange
perfec
an yu get new clothes

But when mi father try
fi teach mi
slide de knife
up to de safeguard thumb

I move de weapon like
a saw inna mi han
an de dyamn rind
break

An if yu have de time
yu can come see mi
in mi ole clothes
peelin

Stumbling down his own oesophagus
he thought he'd check his vitals out.
He found the entrails most illegible,
it wasn't clear what innards were about.

He opted to return to air and light
and certainty; but when he tried
he found the passage blocked; so now
he spends the long day groping there, inside.

CAVE

but further in
a lightbeam
spotted clothing
on the ground
a shirt
that smelt of the man

tracking
along close passages
they picked up
shoes and socks
a vest
his trousers
finally a brief
reminder
smelling of the crutch

and then at last
in a little room
like a cell
at the centre

they found him
huddled naked
in the dark

THEY

they tapped and tapped on the shell
and the shell broke
and the yolk broke

cracked they said it's cracked

then they opened the cracked shell wide
    and cried
              and cried

WINDSCREEN

De garage people
seh de neat
crack in mi windscreen
bound to grow

an though it hardly showin
now, between vibration an de heat
it noh mus grow?

I climb inside
an measure. So I know:
de crack is growin.

WEB

skeins of
perception
catching
light

gossamer
filaments
of radiating
glances

please
do not touch

BIRTHDAYS

The game is metaphor.
'Birthdays: reassuring corners
in the long, dark room of time.'

'Reminder knots,' another voice
proposes. 'Birthdays are reminders
time is heartless, beauty fades.'

There is no string of time
unravelling till the end is cut,
only a dark pool swirling –
letters, matches, galliwasps,
toothpaste tubes and railway tickets,
myriad markers from our lives
in seminal confusion, falsified
by cuckoo-clocks and calendars.

I, celebrating birthdays
in the whirlpool, splutter,
coughing to clear the phlegm.

'Yours, but only partly
yours,' they said.

As if on cue, the poem
shifted in his head.

QUESTION TIME

sometimes a poem
is a mask

to ritualize
connection

& preserve
a little something

shared a little
something treasured

in pretence
that privacy

lives on within
community

There was a young poet
who thrived on his pain
(Hey ho the sun and the rain)
His woman ran off
and he found her again
(Hey ho the sun and the rain)

It pleased him to ask for
a foot in the face
(Hey ho the sun and the rain)
Whenever it hurt enough
words fell in place
(with a Hey ho the sun and the rain)

It happened one summer
nobody knows why
(Hey ho the sun and the rain)
The woman he said he loved
happened to die
(Hey ho the sun and the rain)

He wrote and he wrote
it was his way to grieve
(with a Hey ho the sun and the rain)
The pleasure grief gave him
you wouldn't believe
(Hey ho the sun and the rain)

At length when the sorrow
began to wear thin
(Hey ho the sun and the rain)
He went out and brought
a new torturess in
(Hey ho the sun and the rain)

Turned out she loved him
he found out too late
(Hey ho the sun and the rain)
He's happy as hell
but he cannot create
(Hey ho the sun and the rain)

At every border stood a wall.
But he would not adapt
for anything: that we are trapped
he wouldn't buy at all
until . . .

He burrowed in the dark, a blind
adventurer. He surfaced. Wall behind.
Before him stood another, higher.

THANK-YOU NOTE

first you say
i mustnt write a
routine letter

then photographs
arrive
& photocopies

& you say
tomorrow
tomorrow
i shall write

& then in time you
dont know how
to say i should have
written you before but
this is just to say

GAFFES

We try to smother
troublesome remarks,
but hurtful truths
(however casual) survive,
fluttering tenaciously,
defiantly alive.

DREAM

I dreamt

I grabbed a pail
to dip some water up
to drink

and saw
things floating
in the murk

And then I woke up
thirsty

NOTICE

last week a tripper
drowned

going too far
from shore

the bloated carcass
ran aground
days later

rolled up near
this weather-
beaten notice
here

Dangerous Currents
Beware

beware

MARINERS

who are
the night-cruisers
slicing through dark
dim on the foredeck
scanning for shark

we are
the seafarers
sick in the deep
bilious in daylight
troubled asleep

we are the sea-searchers
scaling the night
keen in the darkness
fish-eyed in light

DIALOGUE FOR ONE

for the NDTC

in this
reflective
exercise

the bodies
imitate

contraction
and release

each
glistening

performing
mirror

honouring
the other

artfully
dancing
identity

THE POND

There was this pond in the village
and little boys, he heard till he was sick,
were not allowed too near.
Unfathomable pool, they said,
that swallowed men and animals just so;
and in its depths, old people said,
swam galliwasps and nameless horrors;
bright boys kept away.

Though drawn so hard by prohibitions,
the small boy, fixed in fear, kept off;
till one wet summer, grass growing lush,
paths muddy, slippery, he found himself
there at the fabled edge.

The brooding pond was dark.
Sudden, escaping cloud, the sun
came bright; and, shimmering in guilt,
he saw his own face peering from the pool.

A READING

Faraway eyes
indifferent as glass

Come with me come
inside the park
there is a fountain
at the centre

Eyes
at last eyes warm

pathways entice

Moving together
eyes holding eyes
we make a journey
both devise

Far
at the centre
the fountain

blooms

STRIPPER

At a sleazy club where strippers are on view
a weary poet stopped for wine
and song; but had to take the stripper too,
whose writhing seemed an image of his line.
She put on clothes to take them off, she wore
performing pieces, such a fuss she made
of skimpy little veils before
her parts (which never were displayed)!
Riddling hard to music, she performed
her teasing art, for which the patron paid.
Nice fleshy legs, gyrating hips that warmed
the watchers; sensuous, lively, educated tits.
The poet looked away, to check the eyes
of grim-faced lechers, soft men going to bits,
suckers deceived by lighting, sold on lies
(while there behind the smoke-dimmed crowd
the cunning pander lurked, a ponce on guard).
She took the last piece off the law allowed.
The poet felt his symbol growing hard.

MUSE

When you woo her
she will fade

This is how
the game is played

     Smilingly
     she leads him on
     He approaches
     Whereupon

     the figure in the
     evening air
     begins to
     slowly disappear

Extraordinary
trade
When you woo her
she will fade

This is how
the game is played

TUTORIAL

'I'm strange,'
you said,
like an apology
with just a hint
of cool defiance.

But you are not
alone, remember;
it is strange inside
the labyrinthine
network wiring
each and every
head, a mess
of shimmering
mirrors,
a surreal forest
of reflection.
You may not
be as different
as you think.

Enjoy, examine
what you find.

Welcome
to the mystery
of mind.

OBLATION

Then shall the poet say:

Draw near, and touch
my suppurating wounds.

This is my psyche
broken for you. Give thanks.

You have not cared enough.
But you may clap.

GARDENING

he planted plenty seed
but where he dropped
a flower weed
would sprout

he pulled the weed out
sowed again
but where he urged
a flower weed came out

despairing
of the strangled flower
he let the dull weed grow
its awkward power

STORYPOEM

well
one day at a concert
with the whole hall full
he entered to vociferous applause
he settled at the keyboard
flexed his fingers
and didn't play
just sat there

listening

EXAMINATION CENTRE

Dilapidated room,
paint peeling.
Sufferers
on edge.

The chief invigilator
gives the word.
The fingered papers rustle.

Outside the centre –
part of my recall –
trees bend and stretch
and breathe.
Winds, playful, tease.

We're struggling here
with questions
and time
and longing
for a life we glimpse
through dust
clouding the panes.

INTERIOR

stuck in there

with the over-stuffed
imported reading-chair

the ritual mask
of native wood

the stereogram
the modish canvasses

a square
glass-fronted

shadow box
revealing

curiosa
locked inside

TUNNEL

Down
on his
belly
in the
tunnel
clawed
the dust
bruising
towards
light
Slow
bellying
dragged
his body
sloughed
the dark

TOASTING A MUSE

One man who came to dinner
wouldn't eat,
just focused on his hostess
instant eloquent devotion.
He'd stand and say, as if proposing
a toast, 'I speak this in your honour,
ma'am, you are so beautiful,'
then chant some passionate verse,
and sit and drink some more
until the spirit moved in him
again, then stand and say
'You are so beautiful' et cetera
and do another item.
Funny fellow. Poet. Mad as hell.

I been there, sort of.
For in that ambience I too
was smitten, by what seemed
to me unusual radiance,
beauty of spirit lighting up the place,
but I kept quiet about it, made small talk,
stayed sober, and enjoyed the food.

WRITING

after Octavio Paz

When in some solitary hour
pen writes on paper
who makes it move?
Who is he writing to, writing for me
this littoral of lips, of dream, this
shoulder to forget the world forever on?

Someone inside me writes, he moves my hand,
selects a word, then pauses, wavering
between green mountains and blue sea.
Coldly examines what I write,
dashes it in the fire.
But this judge is a victim who,
condemning me, condemns himself.
He writes nobody, calls nobody,
he writes himself, gets lost inside himself,
and finds himself again, once more becoming me.

WORKING OUT

a left jab
at the shadow
just inside
his vision

(nothing
there)

a right hook
at the assailant
shaping

(air)

– he's getting fit

and when the real
night finally arrives

he'll come out
of his corner

swinging

SHE

tangling
with undergrowth
he hears

her questioning
the twilight
fears

summoning softly
into jungle
into night

SHADOWS

When the man taps out
a peephole in his crown,
that hole into the dark
pit is for peering down:
but it is hard to tell
what's going on down there:
when shadows thrash
and slither
what we glimpse
are figures either
wrestling for fun or
locked in combat
in a subterranean war.

COUNSELLOR

Reaching out
with irony

she greets
our tensions

registers the timbre
of our screams

MUSEUM PIECE

The thing had wings
that flapped
flapped in the dark of the skull

You let it be they said
we don't care
to know about it
you keep it it is yours

But the thing kept going
flap
flap

So he got himself a lance
and he practiced tilting
tilting

till one day when the thing went flap
he climbed on his practised horse
and galloped into the dark

He rammed the lance in its gullet
and dragged it into the light

then he wiped off the dust and the blood
and he put it on display
(making sure to pin the wings)

DADD, POOR DADD

They said, concerning Richard Dadd,
a delicate talent was all he had;
until, emphatically mad,
he stuck a knife into his dad,
unlocking vision. Sad.

VALLEY PRINCE

for Don Drummond

Me one, way out in the crowd,
I blow the sounds, the pain,
but not a soul
would come inside my world
or tell mi how it true.
I love a melancholy baby,
sweet, with fire in her belly;
and like a spite
the woman turn a whore.
Cool and smooth around the beat
she wake the note inside mi
and I blow mi mind.

Inside here, me one
in the crowd again,
and plenty people
want mi blow it straight.
But straight is not the way; my world
don' go so; that is lie.
Oonoo gi mi back mi trombone, man:
is time to blow mi mind.

ASYLUM

I

a fellow in the madhouse cries
the world is wallowing in lies
innocence is nevermore
the fat worm nestles at the core

II

Fix what you can. Forget the rest.
A little learnt indifference is best.

ZOO STORY

they're grappling for you

the fatuous bourgeois with a book
and the lean wild man

the animal
prowling your territory

the lonely transient
longing

and you

will hold the knife

ENCOUNTER

When I was stumbling
in the dark, confused
and crying out for help,
this friendly fellow seemed amused;

and while I fought like anything
to keep the candle lit
he cheerfully reviewed
the guttering of my wit.

Astonished that the brother found
my struggle such a treat
I turned the flickering light on him
and glimpsed his cloven feet.

CRITIQUE

Yuh a grow, yuh wi come si

Authenticity for you
is blazing revelation,
the suicidal nerve
exposed, the madman
naked in the street.

One day, one day,
if you live long enough,
you'll feel the fire in sobriety,
and come to value
smouldering.

AFTER THE MOVIE

So they all had tea on the ceiling,
                        floating,
high on laughs!

But Mary Poppins flew away,
and the little boy wept in the dark.

Dragged into daylight he is weeping still.

DATA

facts lie
behind the poems
which are true
fictions

THE FOREST

That world I knew was all too plain:
a dry world, crisp and certain
in the sun, where practically anyone
could laugh and prattle all day long,
seeing clear for seeing nothing. But

horrid those grim creatures which, obscure,
lurk in the forest where the leaves
are damp, where sun is filtered
to a nightlight feeble against fears!
Around dark tree-trunks red eyes leer:

> Come; into the forest
> where the leaves are damp,
> where no bird sings. Come,
> flee the sunlit safety of the shore.
> Deep in the forest where the air is dank
> embrace the gracious maggot in the mind.
> The bright boat burns on the beach.

november sunlight
climbing up the shoulders of
the simmering poets

TO TELL THE TRUTH

i used to burn my poems
he said

was troubled
murmuring inside

till puking demons
brought relief

but no one
ever analysed

or even
saw

the stuff
i vomited

i used to burn my poems

Out of the shadow an awkward figure
loomed, commanding, with a gun.
The finger tightened on the trigger.

The finger tightened on the trigger.
She couldn't fight, she couldn't run;
she learned in that peculiar park
how much she feared the gun.

The finger tightened on the trigger.
Then suddenly along the dark
gun-muzzle *whoosh!* a full balloon
came rushing, rainbow-bright!

The awkward figure laughed. And soon
that weird encounter faded into night.

II LOVE IS

WEST INDIAN LOVE SONG

from England

The moon begat our love
the moon on the sea
You said the moon would prove
what love should be

The sea frustrates our love
dissolves my life
The moon that spun our love
sharpens the knife

And to regain my love
I'll ride the sea
I'll put my arms about the moon
and we'll be free

A TEMPERATE LOVE POEM

Hoarfrost glimmering beyond
latched windows. Icicles
adorning iron bars. Inside
we are cold, or colder than
we like it, snuggling
each other, hopefully.

Some fine day, spring
(as in a poem) will burst
again, real sun
shine for true, and we
won't need each other so;
then may we choose to share
the summer warmth and live
together, happily apart.

DREAMTIME

the lady dreams
herself shut out
her lord in the castle
his lady without

he waves from a window
a long way away
she doesn't know what
he intends to convey

one evening in dreamtime
the wind blew right
and a voice floated down
from that worrying height

i live in a castle
with very thick walls
and the drawbridge drawn
up tight

THE REASSURANCE

When, my sweet,
the man taps out
a peephole in his crown,
that hole into the pit's
for peering down.

But watch! – the dark forms
floundering, flapping,
slithering,
have not dethroned
the previous person
you have owned;
the person still
is what the person seems;
no pressing need to shrink
from fictive monsters
flailing at your dreams.

Bask in the present minutes:
he
uncorked by patient love
pours tonic constancy
(though pits brood fearful
since that foetid day
another man, your father,
slipped away).

Drink: and accept
the offered peephole in the mind.
You must not shrink,
no matter how the shadows thrash
or crawl.
Pull away, or blink,
and you will never
own him
all.

TOGETHERNESS

I

Lying in the dark together
we
in wordless dialogue
defined community.

II

You switch the light on to inspect
an alien remark.
And now your body stutters.

No more lying in the dark.

A VOYAGE

'Beware, beware their evil song:
they eat your flesh,
they bleach your bones,
you won't last long.'

His vessel neared an island.
Shimmering calm. Air still.
Enthralling song
across the green sea floating

paralysed his will.

O heaven within his reach,
he felt. And swam for shore.

His fortune waited, lolling on the beach.

WOMANSONG

i am sinking
do you care
i am drowning
over here

throw a lifeline
out for me
drag my body
from the sea

i am dying
can't you see
that girl lying
there is me

lying dying
here on shore
i don't know you
anymore

CRITIC

Questions about meaning
really concern you now
whose deconstruction, exquisite
unravelling, terrorised.
You were in control.

Did you misread her eyes
when, leafing through a magazine
in bed, she glanced your way?

Unstable text, your wife
has broken up the game.
Now she has left you, academic
reading doesn't seem the same.

VERSION

'A marvellous otaheite
dark and sweet,'
the Lord said. 'Eat;
and every time you go to it
the apple will be whole.'
Adam loved the apple
heart and soul

until he fancied
on another tree
another apple, dark
(and sweet, presumably).
He checked it.
he enjoyed the change,
the pleasure of the new fruit
succulent and strange.

Eventually remembering
his sweet original,
he turned again and found
a change more radical:
he bit it, and a huge hole gaped:
the thing had lost its power:
his luscious apple now
was withering and sour.

WORKSHOP

he casually decodes
her scrambled mews
the cat is reading
heat

miaow implodes

a molotov
well mixed

o she will have him
she will have him
fixed

SHORT STORY

I

How carefully they walk
together, hardly ever touching.
Neither he nor she is rushing
into anything.

But something's going on
beneath the easy talk
of books & family & friends.
Read on.

II

They're in a private place
together, searching
through the story, getting to know
the characters, intertwining
themes, discretion & desire,
exploring conflict, complication,
restructuring lives
in the imagination.

III

Goodbye. 'Let's keep in touch,'
they say, without conviction.
They hug each other warmly, and depart.
But each has nestled in the other's art,
so it's another story in the fiction.

MEMENTO

a wrinkled head
carved sideways
on a hump

a wooden figure
old as sin

it fell from me

& the old man
broke his neck

i left the pieces
  in the garbage
at the railway station

RIDING HOOD: VERSION

he seemed a proper granny
till she grasped the truth –

beneath the pretty bonnet
lay a well-hung youth

working up a story
that he wanted read

with the happy ending
of her maidenhead

ENDGAME

She knew
the risk

but played
the fool

just entering
his eyes

then trying
to run away.

Too late.
Checkmate.

CASANOVA

Flaunting his gym-toned pectorals,
washboard stomach, fashion-
conscious locks, he worked the image
of philanderer, every woman's
fantasy or threat.

But something tremulous inside
his gravelly baritone exposed
a small boy quivering in the dark,
his mother dead, his father gone away,
groping for explanations.

HAPPY HOUR

her laughter quivers
like a flimsy bridge
before it breaks

her laughter covers up
a hole
and sharpened stakes

but the detested animal
is potent still it seems

the prepossessing monster
dominates her dreams

MOMENT OF TRUTH

as both were
always listening
for what was being said
inside civilities

the genial courtesies
did not drown out
their body language
whispering exchange

and they maintained the dialogue
sotto voce many months
until the clash of glances
the electrifying flash

PEACETIME

bomb-disposal
combed the area
& declared it clean

but love i cannot
guarantee
safe conduct

through the rubble
of my dreams –

i've read
too many people
blown to bits

by land mines
lying silent
in the dust

long after
all those bells
& all that joy

long after solemn treaties
had been signed & sealed

SNAPSHOT

i press your eyes
and study the exposure
in my head
i have you
sagging in a rumpled bed
(don't go don't go)

one snapshot
in the miles & miles
of undeveloped
yesterdays

(shutter your gaze)

A MEMORY

Not a cloud in sight:
day calm and bright:
cliché tranquillity.

Out of the blue she floated in,
a memory,
playing her enigmatic grin

(whose legend reads 'At last, at last'
but is re-written fast
as you move in):

nostalgic, but embarrassing.
I mumbled 'Hi' and moved away.

A ghost I'll never lay.

PANTOMIME

She smiled and smiled and seemed to be
the genial friend, the keen collaborator
until the transformation scene; then she
became a block of stone, a champion hater.

PERSEPHONE

i sleep & wake
& see the dream again –

the spectre
of my youthful paramour

my profiling adonis
begging to be gored

my faithless lover cruising
at the cemetery gate

NIGHT FLIGHT

He's off into the night
alone, the lucky devil –
no one hanging on his tail
to keep him out of trouble.

He flaps his wings
in the uncaged air
and, floating on the night,
is gliding everywhere,

is revelling in flight –
until he feels
the fish-hook in the flesh,
the line tugged tight.

DIALOGUE FOR DANCERS

for the NDTC

I

at home on stage
his wife the martyr
bleeds

II

the other woman
wraps a sensuous leg

III

torn
between

his clinging wife's
domestic harmonies
the open breakfast face

and that sleek wanton queen
the red rose in her hair

his wanting body
writhes

PARLOUR GAME

Antennae register
enticement, picking up
glances and the enigmatic
smile.

Superfly is tripping
into trouble, visioning
himself entangled
in her script.

STORYBOARD

Love gave her eyes:
the tough man snatched,
locked them up tight.

Love gave her hand:
the tough man tickled it
early one night.

Love gave her tongue:
the tough man found
it tasted right.

Love gave her body:
the tough man smiled,
switched off the light.

Love gave her heart:
the tough man tensed,
ready for flight.

REUNION

long long ago
we heard the eyes
vote *no*

not here
not yet
not ever

but the whirligig
of time
has brought us round

years after
that brief pantomime

and we are playing
new games now

acknowledging the strain
of lust inside our laughter

AN OFFERING

In love, and reverently inclined,
I bear the lesions of my mind.
But from your eyes the message is
that I must do the bandages
again, swaddle my wounds.

Such prophylactic fear impugns
my gift. Unwrap my injuries.

In spite of love
desire to be alone
haunts him like prophecy.

Observe: the baby chuckles,
gurgles his delight
that daddy-man is handy,
to be stared at, clawed at,
spitted-up upon;
the baby's elder brother
laughs, or hugs, and nags
for popcorn or a pencil
or a trip.

And see: the frazzled wife
who jealously
protects the idol infant
from the smallest chance
of harm, and anxious
in the middle of the night
wakes up to coughs; and checks,
and loves, and screams
her nerves; but loves him
patient still: the wife
who sweets the bigger boy
and teases him through homework,
bright as play.

But you may not observe
(it is a private sanctuary)
the steady glowing power
that makes a man feel loved,
feel needed, all of time;
yet frees him, king of her
emotions, jockey of her
flesh, to cherish
his own corner
of the cage.

In spite of love
this dream:
to go alone
to where
the fishing boats are empty
on the beach
and no one knows
which man is
father, husband, victim,
king, the master of one cage.

LOVE IS

a giving
& a measured taking

amputation
re-creating

everlasting
interface

a prison
& an open space

a teasing glimpse
of holy grail

a generator
that can fail

the naked jugular
the knife

the torsion
balance in my life

NORTH COAST HOTEL

the lovely pregnant lady
leaning on the disco bar
lets dancehall flow
through her

an elegant
black patrician
breaking out

before her man
a chunky brother
decorously sipping wine

while she is moving
like a native to the bass
teaching the child
dancehall

FOR A SON

Watching you swell
your mother's womb, only a crude
connection seemed to make itself.
Watching your mother swell, with having you,
taught tenderness, for she
while growing you was all my care,
happy as she rounded.
Even alive and howling clear
you seemed a thing your mother had.

But you yourself I learnt
could make me feel – maybe your laugh,
that warm primordial gurgle, did it:
your personal self enjoined my love,
tying our lives as with the living cord.

Be strong my bond and my release
from time. Be tall, stretch separate; and know
the love you've nourished though you may not care.

LITTLE BOY CRYING

Your mouth contorting in brief spite and hurt,
your laughter metamorphosed into howls,
your frame so recently relaxed now tight
with three-year-old frustration, your bright eyes
swimming tears, splashing your bare feet,
you stand there angling for a moment's hint
of guilt or sorrow for the quick slap struck.

The ogre towers above you, that grim giant,
empty of feeling, a colossal cruel,
soon victim of the tale's conclusion, dead
at last. You hate him, you imagine
chopping clean the tree he's scrambling down
or plotting deeper pits to trap him in.

You cannot understand, not yet,
the hurt your easy tears can scald him with,
nor guess the wavering hidden behind that mask.
This fierce man longs to lift you, curb your sadness
with piggy-back or bull-fight, anything,
but dare not ruin the lessons you should learn.

You must not make a plaything of the rain.

PALIMPSEST

Grandma, much younger
than her age-paper,
is giggling on the floor
with baby Jon
as with his daddy
forty years ago. 'Age
is just a number,'
as the slogan says.

Grandpa, seeming
buried in a book,
gives thanks for her
endearing gift
and mumbles Larkin,
'What will survive of us
is love.'

AT HOME

I

No strangers here
tonight: alone at last
with music
we reclaim our home
we rediscover space
we do not need to speak

II

This evening no one raps.
Our music underscores
the vacancy, the walls
demand possession. O
such gaps! This quiet
evening palls.

GAMES

Sometimes
when he teetered
on the brink

the woman
saddled with
his mind

would wish him dead
then pray
he'd come again
to safety
and her bed

Time after time
he sidled back
into her care

contending
there was nothing
in the world
to fear

INTERLUDE

Life of the party, he's
a clown on springs

until the keeper
puts him down.

Jack in the box
again, recoiling.

Quick, now!
Click.

EPIPHANY

your eyes
bright headlights
dip

& we flash by –

SEEN

beyond the longing
& the lies

half-hidden in
equivocating eyes

(be careful
if you can't be good)

a lurking dread
of being

understood

SISTER

beneath the undulating
calm
dark currents move

recalling
hurt & rage
& fracture

o my romantic soul
sister longing
for a whole

new world of love
i hear your soft song
breaking on the page

ACROBAT

brave woman

trusting
he has gauged

her arc
exactly

she's letting go
she's flying

in the dark

GIVE T'ANKS

Anodda year of love.
Give t'anks. An' pray
dat God-Above
will seh to time, No way,
No way:
de word is love.

THE PLEDGE

I

She's black
and beautiful
you lucky nigger
poet sing

II

I love her
black I love
her sensual
grace

I love her
black I love
her bright
enquiring face

digging truth
beyond my eyes
weeding dark lies

I love her black

III

but she says No
Stay with with me nigger
lover keep it true
Say with me nigger

I love her
    (*love her*)
Also we are black
        (*are black*)
        (*are black*)

SHE TELLS HERSELF

Something like love
is hiding deep inside

the silences.

He doesn't often talk
to me. I trawl

his eyes.

There is a place inside me
not even you will ever see

I locked my wound away
the day I saw the roses wither

I will not call the name
of the deceitful brother

I locked my wound away
the day I saw the roses wither

INTERFACE

Discombobulated
by his riddling eyes,
the foxy lady tries
to seem untouched, but may
have seriously miscalculated.
The predator can sense
her willingness to end her
laughable pretence.
She wants to play
surrender.

That boy who loved you
(and you loved him but never told him so)
has scrawled his epitaph on your pink vellum.

The girl whom you detested (and who knew)
has paid you back – with troubling ambiguity,
neatly on the back side of your best friend's
witty retching.

The lad you asked just to be kind
has pulled a big surprise, has written
something shrewd yet generous to a fault.

This album
is a mine field floating,
waiting to sink your craft.

MOTH

A somewhat intellectual moth,
she could dilate for hours on flame
and how to fight desire.
She'd read an awful lot on fire,
but it consumed her just the same.

INTERVIEW

he sits there
looking thoughtful
slyly taking me in

from top to bottom
eyes / bust / legs

meandering
through the detail
of my life & times
simpatico

but i can feel
the charge
that he does not
acknowledge

i know he knows i see
the amber light

& will not cross
the bridge

PROPOSITION ONE

A routine love that hangs its hat
on coming home and wipes its feet
precisely every afternoon, and greets
its wife with proper peck and asks
how went the day, is not for me.
Love will not set the clock
by my affections
and wind its own springs up
in time.

To keep the thing alive
let's loosen up,
let's improvise, my love,
relax, be casual, enjoy the lime,
relinquish the habitual,
reshape the paradigm.

THE LOVERS

after René Magritte

The lovers kissing
do not see
each other, do not feel
unmediated hair and skin.

Each hooded
in an opaque swirl,
neither seems aware
of something strange.

Do not disturb.
They are in love.
Each feels a kinship
with the other's mask.

OPERATION

after a thorough
physical

he dug a hole
into her skull

he cut
a great big window
in her gut

then mumbling how
he was so sorry but
he couldn't stay

the fucker
walked away

HOME

Father, given a chance to be
away a while, be free
a month or two,
was quick to grab it!

But freedom's
neither here nor there:
home is the habit
he will always wear.

ANOTHER WEDDING

The ritual is well-known:
the bridegroom says his total vows,
the bride says hers,
the clergyman declares how strong love is.

Yet, each time, something stirs:

they resurrect our own
promises
promises

DEPARTURE LOUNGE

The young man,
when the flight is called,
is blowing his nose to clear
the sadness of departure.
The girl who's leaving looks
composed. They're travelling
on different planes
to different destinations.

Partir,
c'est mourir un peu.
Time after time
these moments
devastate.

But partings down the years
have helped to make me
ready to say goodbye.

BREAKING UP

Stay away she told me
Don't come back

It's time
to turn the page

Refocused now she
doesn't take my calls

she blocks
heartbroken messages

but can't delete
our history

her eyes a secret garden
her touch a sacrament

PUSSYCAT

His conversation flattered; she said yes
and went the way his thoughts inclined;
but not content with rooting in the flesh
he stuck an amorous finger in her mind;
and now her mind lies naked to his pleasure
and hungry for possession, she's afraid.
She would have barred him from her treasure
if she had known her mind was getting laid.

GUINEA PIG

susceptible
to viruses

that bother
human beings

& therefore
used

as a laboratory
animal

he seldom
bites

he's almost
human:

gentle
stupid

animal
caged

WHY, THIS IS HULL

on a grey day
(spring) when

on my balcony
beyond plate glass

pigeons
flutter & strut

i wing
a little something

to my sun

PRESENCES

You're here.
I conjure you
house-coated, half-asleep
in the armchair by the window.

Awake in bed
I hug you, memory.
They who one another keep
Alive, ne'er parted be.

Clinton and Barbara,
you stand accused
of Christian practices,
of faith in God and helpfulness
to people. You habitually buoy
us up with cheerfulness, which is
the very heart of your offence:
your challenge to a world of friction,
the marvel of your unaffected joy.

In view of all the evidence,
we vote for your conviction.

Clinton and Barbara,
you shall serve hereafter
another forty years
of love and laughter.

III   ON HOLY WEEK

a sequence for radio

Beware: the following secular depiction
of people living through the Crucifixion
revises Holy Writ. The gospel story triggers
the maker's thinking about various figures:
he offers moments, voices, attitudes;
and if, occasionally, faith intrudes
don't blame the maker, blame the borrowed bible
(for humanist agnostics, unreliable).

The maker who presents these versions
is grateful, in advance, to all those persons
(including The Almighty) who'll forgive him
his ordinary rhyme and rhythm,
allow each portrait arguably true,
and kindly authorize invention too.

Now hear these people. Some are good.
Some fail to do the things they should;
but hear them all. Let each one speak
a little of Unholy Week.

JESUS IN GETHSEMANE

I

O Father – if it be thy will –
let this cup pass from me.
But o my Father, I submit to thee:
use me, thy servant, still.

II

Father, I cannot drink this cup!
Release me (if it be thy will).
Unwilling, Father, I am still
thy servant. Bear me up.

A PRIEST

The chap's a madman rather than a liar:
I think he's quite convinced he's The Messiah!
That God might be a carpenter! Absurd!
It's quite the silliest nonsense I have heard!
(You know my bias; but) a priest –
perhaps an elder, at the very least –
would seem to be more likely for the job
than some untutored Galilean yob!

JUDAS

That evening, not so long ago,
the Master, fingers in the dish,
said gently: 'Did I not choose
you twelve, yet one of you's
a devil?' Mocking, he glanced
at me; and others, quick
on cue, looked my way too.
The odd man out is always
Judas. 'We're from Galilee.'
(Nasty little province,
smells of fish!)

The point is,
Jesus never trusted me.
John, who's favourite, he's
from Galilee. Like Peter,
Andrew, all the cosy band.
Which Galilean, Lord,
will sit at your right hand?

Tonight I kissed him
and I saw
that mocking glance again.
'Betrayest thou the Master
with a kiss?' he said, ironic; then
seemed pleased or something
like relieved he'd got me
right. That knowing judge of men,
he surely ought to realize
that truths are often complicated:
what he spotted he created,
distrusting with those distant
foreign eyes.

The point is not the money, I'll
go give it back. For, hell,
what's thirty bits of silver?
I would not sell
the Master, he's for free. Just
preserve my purity of hate
for him I served and loved so well.
My Lord, the Master of my fate,
always withheld his trust.

I dreamt us strolling, arm in loving arm,
along the avenue that skirts the border;
our tender courting days wheeled back.
Just then we heard a yapping,
loud, a pack in full pursuit!

Into our lives he crashed,
a lamb, bleeding and bruised,
and weary with the chase.
I picked him up and cuddled him
in my warm arms, my newest baby boy.

The hounds were yelping louder,
nuzzling the hedge. And then
(but why? but why?) you snatched
the poor thing from my arms,
and with 'We must not interfere,
my love, the dogs demand their prey,'
you tossed their quarry over
the prickly hedge. The ravenous pack
were through him in an instant,
ravaging the body.

That moment, in my dream,
our sweet love died; that afternoon
I sat alone, playing with thorns.
At length, I turned to you
to plead forgiveness.
You offered that, and love;
but, broken in simple grief,
I could not take your proffered
bread and wine.

PILATE

And then I tried to pass the buck;
but Herod, with astute aplomb,
politely, sent him back.

I tried to move the people
to accept he might be freed
this feast of The Passover.
'Kill him! Kill him! Nail him
to the cross!' They clamoured for
Barabbas, insurrectionist, a bandit
who's attacked imperial rule.
'Try Jesus for yourselves,' I told the mob;
'You judge him by your law.'
'Kill him!' they hollered louder,
'Nail him to the cross!'

Then slimy priests, those holy rogues
of politics, began to turn the screws:
'You must not fail to sentence Christ,
soi-disant King of Jews.
Your masters wouldn't like it much
if we should let them know
we caught a man supplanting Rome
and you have let him go.'

My basic job is keeping peace
and reverence for Rome. The man
was bad for both. I had to yield.
'I find no fault in him,' I cried,
and ordered water brought;
and, public gesture of defeat
(sound politics, I thought),

I washed these loving
histrionic hands.
The crowd surprised me, seized
the guilt of their demands.

                    You know
I am not weak. I could, I would
stand up for Jesus if I thought
that were the thing to do. Now
he is dead. He didn't seem to care,
so why should you? How is your head,
my sweet?

PETER

O Jesus, you were right:
I have denied you, Lord; in spite
of protestation, failed
the test.

             When that girl hailed
me, Lord, I should have hollered loud,
'He's God I follow!', Lord, and faced the crowd.
For all my talk, somehow
I couldn't then; it's too late now:
the deed is done, and twice the cock has crowed.
O Lord, more than this worthless life I owed
to you who made the world make sense!

Though hard on overconfidence,
you taught that fear is lack of faith, is sin;
yet I denied you, Lord, to save my skin.
These bitter tears won't wash away the stain.

But o my Jesus, let me try again:
make me, as promised, your foundation rock;
forgive me, Lord, and I will feed your flock.

SOLDIERS

Hey! Boy! If you are God
then say who spit on you!
Say who, you bloody fraud!

We're gonna nail you, Lord!

SIMON OF CYRENE

Why me? It's
just my luck.
Another great
procession
coming through,
some carpenter
called Christ.
Women weeping,
people jeering,
and the Roman
soldiers hard
and cold, 'Hey, you!
Not me? 'Hey! You!'
I didn't figure.
'Take this cross!'
Orders is orders
from a Roman guard.
I'm strong enough,
and this man Christ
is weary, bleeding,
scourged so deep.

Wicked heavy
heavy load,
the cross I bore
for Jesus. 'King
of Jews' the sign said.
Rubbish. Wonder what
he'd done?

A WOMAN NAMED MARY

We get a good view here.

I know that man.
It's Jesus! I've anointed him –
in Bethany, I think: at Simon's house.
A lovely piece of man; real sweet.
Those hands. That mouth. Those feet.
Some stingy bastard tried to say
the money spent on nard was waste,
and should have gone to help the poor!
Jesus spoke up for me.

JESUS ON THE ROAD

Weep not for me but for yourselves
and all the world to come. For some
shall bless their barren luck
that they have never given suck;
and they shall pray the mountain fall
and hide them from the sky.
Such evil, and the tree is green;
much more when it is dry.

MALEFACTOR (LEFT)

So you is God?
Den teck wi down! Tiefin doan bad
like crucifyin!
Wha do you, man?
Save all a wi from dyin!

MALEFACTOR (RIGHT)

Doan bodder widdim, Master; him
must die;
but when you kingdom come, remember I.
When you sail across de sea,
O God of Judah, carry I wit dee.

CENTURION

I've seen it often:
when the pain gets harsh,
the fellow up there on the cross
will often cry for mercy. Usually
if he is lucid he will curse.
Sometimes when the pain gets harsh
the victim stop proclaiming
he is innocent,
and swears revenge.
But this man's different: he forgave
the people who enjoyed his pain!
Never nailed a man like this before.
Surely this man was God.

MARY (MOTHER)

To see him
strung up there
between two robbers,
scorned, abused!

I still remember when
an angel, as they say,
predicted him;
and Joseph; and those
tough uncomfortable
miles to Bethlehem;
and bedding in a stable,
for the inn was full;
and giving birth.

O God, the pain!
To hear him cry! To see
the head fall slack!
The wounded hands! The spear-slit
in his side!

JOHN

I fished; but he was deep.
The perfect man. Divine.
His love
was everlastingly benign.

Stripped there,
broken on the cross:
perfection sacrificed!
O help us to endure our loss,
blessed body of Christ.

JOSEPH OF ARIMATHAEA

Sometimes, avoiding trouble, we accept defeat.
(Painful sometimes, being discreet.)

Soon Sabbath now. The corpse of Christ
ought to come down by then.
Which means pulling strings again.
I think I'll bury him where I
had planned to have my own bones lie.

Thank God there's something I can do.
Forgive me, Lord, for not proclaiming you.

MARY MAGDALENE

Me, crying; just outside the tomb.
This fellow asks me why I'm crying.
I ask him where the body is.
'Mary,' the man says quietly.

I turn.
            The voice is His.

THOMAS

Sure, I'm lacking faith. It's just
I am not gullible like some.
Better to be wrong than dumb.

There is no doubt
I loved the King of Men.
But if he seem to come again
some simple test must be applied:
I'll plunge these fingers in his riven side
to know, first-hand, that what I see
is him that died.

Doubt's my creed:
till time breeds proof
sand seems more honest than rock.
If my Lord lives, he'll meet the need
of those who question, those who mock;
of us who, wanting faith, will stand aloof.

IV TIME COME

A CONFERENCE HYMN

for Anglican Consultative
Council Meeting, May 2009

Lord of our diversity,
unite us all, we pray;
welcome us to fellowship
in your inclusive way.

Teach us all to have respect;
to love, and not deride.
Save us from the challenges
of selfishness and pride.

Sanctify our listening
and help us get the sense
of each perplexing argument
before we take offence.

Teach us that opinions which
at first may seem quite strange
may reflect the glory of
your great creative range.

May the Holy Spirit now
show us the way preferred.
May we follow the commands
of your authentic Word.

RECREATION

He didn't spend six whole days on the world,
he made it in a single night
when things were not going well and, having hurled
some earnest failures into the abyss,
he poured himself some nectar and created this,
a funny thing he figured was all right.

HOMILY

He seemed forever full of fun –
witty, audacious Anglican
who hardly ever met a pun
he wouldn't entertain.

Shared laughter is the main
thing I recall, but now and then
he could turn serious, like when

'I'm sorry if I seem to be accusing you,'
he said, 'of not discriminating as you should;
but sometimes when the Devil is amusing
you seem to be forgetting he's no good.
Remember: goodness matters.'

A message from his pastoral core.

Beyond the grace of humour
there is more.

TRANSITIONS

for Alli & Joyce

In church triumphant
only months ago
he gave away the prize

but now at Eastertide
the father of the bride
is dead

bequeathing us
perpetual open house
a family of friends

and willing us to rise
above our sorrows
and terrestrial ends

AT CHURCH

the old man
stumbles in
a grisly sermon
DEATH
THE ULTIMATE
EXAM   stop writing   time

beyond him
stained glass
morning sun
the risen Christ
and two or three
apostles

PRAISE THE LORD

full tabernacle
shouting to the shimmy of
wicked tambourines

COMMUNION

eyes no longer
altar-focused
light upon
a ragged stranger
peering through
a window at the side

and monitor
what we perceive
as a potential threat

a robber maybe
or a man unhinged
who probably
will crash the service
and disturb the peace

unless he is
an angel

EVE

the garden
seemed

a proper
paradise

until
she buck up

on a serpent
talking nice

IN THE GARDEN

Until the fascinating snake
she didn't know, she didn't want to know.

But when the serpent, tired of being eyed,
unwreathed himself to go,
Eve yielded. 'No,' she cried,
'I'll have a taste.' And so . . .

MOTHER OF JUDAS, MOTHER OF GOD

for Sheila Barnett & the NDTC

Curtain.
Kettledrum.
Two women meet
in an empty place.

The traitor's mother, jittery,
darting behind her grief,
explores
the calm authority of love.

She understands, she knows,
an inner voice
advises. *Give.*
And gradually

vibrations, bond
of blood, the shawl
transfigured,
canopy.

The women grieve together
now, acknowledging
the sanguine promise
of the cross.

Crescendo.
Fade.
A rope hangs
from the tree.

BOARDING SCHOOL

Saturday is pictures evening,
chairs are carried to the gym;
happy little boys enquire
'Who is in it?' 'What's the flim?'
'What's the flim? And who is in it?
Rita Hayworth? Doris Day?'
With a whirr the old projector
wafts excited boys away.

Do not let that tricky bastard
touch your treasure, you damn fool!
Spurn the dawg! Humiliate him!
Tie a tin can to his tool!
Come with me instead, I beg you;
trust me, I will treat you right.
Sexy-body, Nice-gal, Sweetness,
climb the stairs with me tonight.

Sunday morning: to the chapel
after breakfast off we go,
dressed to kill in suit and tie
(we're extras in the Sunday show),
to pray and otherwise perform
as reverential prodigies,
sing the hymns and look fulfilled,
no matter what the message is.

Can the preacher counteract
the awesome power of Hollywood?
Has he seen Delilah dancing?
Does he know her legs are good?
Who's he talking to, I wonder.
Does he know the flesh is sweet?
Does he know that wine's for drinking?
Does he know that bread's to eat?

HOUSEMASTER AT WORK

Bend, boy, bend: *a dog's*
obey'd in office. Bend.
Empty your pockets, please,
and touch your toes.

I am the system, boy: authority:
the master, guardian of roles.
Behave, or suffer.
Bend now, bend.

Other routines obscure
this fundamental.
Prayers, classes,
lunchtime, tea,
house matches, prep,
a beer, an argument
about the team,
the piles of books
we have to mark,
distract us from the stark
brutality of our regime.
Robes and furr'd gowns hide all.

TO A CRIPPLED SCHOOLMASTER

Your study doubled as a Common Room,
with billiards, laughter, loud debate;
and if some little cretin went too far
your magisterial wit would set him straight.

I still recall your dragging up the stairs,
allowing travel time before each bell;
I liked your funny classes (though in truth
I really cannot claim you taught us well).

We watched you crawl from bad to worse,
drag slower and slower until the term
you didn't walk: your classes came
to see you fade from ailing to infirm.

When you retired from teaching, as you had to –
your body wouldn't serve your driving will –
we built a special house to cage you in
so anyone could come and see you still.

The few occasions when I looked you up
I saw a living carcass wasting slow,
that sprightliness of mind a crudish irony
when all your wretched limbs were withering so.

Without a conscious plan to be neglectful
I didn't seem to find the time
to drop in for your running commentary
on what you called 'the national pantomime'.

I wonder whether time has stolen from me
something that matters deeply (or should do)
and whether anything I manage now will ever
relieve my guilt about neglecting you.

And when you die I know I shall be sorry,
remembering your kindness. But the fear
of facing death stops me from coming
to see you dying smiling in your chair.

OUTING

A rush of boys reporting in.
Enquiry, and a hush.

'Drowned, drowned, Marriott is drowned.'

That curious thirst for detail swells;
in waves the teachers rise
like undertakers
and descend the cold stone steps.

THE CASTLE

His mother told him of the king's
enormous thick-walled castle where
with lots of yellow courtiers
he kept his yellow court of fear.

The bold knight hopped a milk-white horse,
spurred fiercely, keen as anything;
resolved, this honourable knight,
to slay that fearful king.

The giddy knight rode hard and fast.
At dusk he heaved a dreadful sigh:
at last, that frightful yellow flag
against the darkening sky!

Living is Fearing. Tired, he read
the writing on the castle wall,
and braced himself to slay that king
who terrifies us all.

The drawbridge down, the knight spurred hard,
galloping into battle;
but as he neared, the bridge pulled up
with a disdainful rattle.

Too late to stop, he took the plunge;
accoutred well, he couldn't float;
and, loud exclaiming 'Death to Fear!',
he drowned himself in the moat.

HERITAGE

whispering ancestors
enfold me in their loving
ghostly immanence

LITERARY EVENING, JAMAICA

In a dusty old crumbling building just fit for rats
and much too large for precious poetry circles
the culture fans sat scattered in the first ten rows
listening for English poetry.

Geoff read Larkin beautifully, Enright too,
and Michael Saunders talked between the poems:
'I don't say they are wonderful,' he said,
'and would not say that anybody says
they're great. I offer them
as two fair English poets writing nowadays.
They're anti-gesture, anti-flatulence,
they speak their quiet honesties without pretence.'

The longer section of the evening's programme
was poems by the locals, undergraduates,
some coarse, some wild, and many violent,
all bloody with the strains of rape and childbirth,
screaming hot curses anti-slavery,
'Down with the limey bastards! Up the blacks!
Chr-rist! Let's tear the painted paper
off all the blasted cracks!'

The more I heard the more it seemed
a pretty rotten choice to read us Larkin,
dull-mannered, scared, regressive Phil,
saying No to everything or Soon, Not Yet.
So many bulging poets must have blushed
and wondered where the hell they'd ever get
with noisy poems, brash, self-conscious, colourful,
and feared that maybe they were born too crude.
Maybe they were; but it was bloody rude

seeming to ask for things that don't belong out here
where sun shines hot and love is plentiful.

For to us standing here, a naked nation
bracing ourselves for blows, what use
is fearfulness and bland negation?
What now if honesty should choose
to say, in all this world's confusion,
that we are still too young for disillusion?

JAMAICA 1979

a stone's throw
from the revolutionary
slogans on the wall

an old black woman
scavenging
in ruins

Cars idle
at the traffic lights
waiting for green

REPRISE

What now if honesty should choose
to say, in all this world's confusion,
that we are still too young for disillusion?

Well, that was 1962.

And here we are, a fractured nation
jumping up in celebration
of fifty years of chattering pretence
at independence,

though decades of political confusion
have made the growing rough,
and we're now old enough
for disillusion.

THE ROACHES

We had a home. The roaches came
to stay. They spread until they had control
of kitchen, pantry, study, then the whole
damned house. We fought them, but the game
was set. We sprayed, and they kept breeding all the same.

We found a house with plenty space,
clean and dry and full of light.
We checked beneath the sink – no roach in sight.
We checked the cupboards – not a trace
of roaches. No roach anyplace.

And so we moved.
                    The roaches came.
We sprayed, but they kept breeding all the same.

Mine history
for the energy it frees.

Do not spend precious time
hanging from family trees.

Time and the changing passions played them tricks,
Killing the shop-soiled resolutions dead.
Gone are the early angry promises
Of rich men squeezed, of capitalists bled.
More adult honesties have straightened ties
And brushed the dinner-jackets clean,
Maturer minds have smelt out fallacies
And redefined what thinkers mean.

Hope drives a chromium symbol now
And smiles a toothpaste passion to the poor,
With colder eloquence explaining how
The young were foolish when they swore
They'd see those dunghills dank and dreary
All replaced by bright new flats:
Good sense was never youthful fury
And rash young promises by brats . . .

'Let's drink a loyal toast to dedication:
We mean the same but youth is past;
We are the fathers of our nation,
The thinking leaders come at last.
Cheers for the faith of simple minds,
Cheers for the love of humble friends;
Love does not alter when it finds
That we have redefined its ends.'

THE MILITANT

was into painting
butterflies

& now
is into jackboots

stomping painters
painting butterflies

MAVERICK

They charged him with a lack of guts
and still he wouldn't do as they desired;
to all their quick solutions offering buts
instead of the agreement they required.

They dropped him from the inner group,
achieving thus consensus of a fashion.
The relics were a loyal troop
who could be certified for passion.

GROUNATION

for Cedric Brooks

out of that pain
that bondage
heavy heavy sounds
our brothers' weary march
our shackled trip

a joyful horn takes off
to freedom time
remembered & foretold

Release I brother let me go
let my people go
home to Ethiopia
in the mind

MUNTU

for Janheinz Jahn

My ancestors
alive inside the daylight
closed up invisible in air
float from the pages of your book.
We called their names.

Enter my father, laughing,
a gregarious black.
Behind him his black father,
formidable, stern.
Fathers who fathered me.

My mother's mother shuffles in,
dragging her gentleness along the glare.
She indicates her father,
who looks white.
I start to hear the irons clink.
He dissipates my terror with a wink.

The language they're conducted in
dictates the play in these debates.
Good english, as they say, discriminates.
White people language white as sin.

FOR QUEEN ELIZABETH II

Longest reigning British Head of State
(September 2015)

You have been Jamaica's
Head of State
till now
Your Majesty

But it is not
in ceremonial fealty
we salute

this latest marker
in your life

It is in recognition
of exemplary
performance
in a role

that was not yours
before the day
you learnt you really
might inherit a throne

We celebrate
your dignified embrace
of duty all these years

and your perennial
graciousness

MONTAGE

England, autumn, dusk –
so different from that quarter-hour
at home when darkness drops:
there's no flamboyant fireball
laughing a promise to return;
only a muted, lingering farewell,
and day has passed to evening.

HEY, REF!

Not long ago
that godlike player
dribbled round each obstacle
or shoulder-charged like stone.
Now time is marking him.
Hey, Ref, that's foul!

Play on.

Beyond the touchline,
flabby, bent,
more ancient idols watch
and wait.

The whistle blows. Full time.

TOURNAMENT

Nostalgic devils 'playing for fun'
in their declining years,
they scramble till the match is done
and smile as if to say, 'Who cares?'

That loser, sweltering
in bed, contending with a sheet,
he cares. He's grappling
with midnight memories of defeat.

TO AN INTERVIEWER

for Usain Bolt

Greatness
is to false-start
an to feel di world
stop dead

Mi draw mi shirt off
leave di track
an watch di race
in shock

Greatness is to look
inside
di failure
try mi best
to swallow up di pain

Greatness is
to get mi head to settle
on di nex event

run right dis time
an hear di stadium
goh wild

SWIMMER

That powerful swimmer
furrowing the pool
towards the final wall . . .

Mourn him, the crumpled athlete:
his element was water;
now they'll sink him
in the ground, he's gone
to rust, that muscled plough.

UNIVERSITY STUDY

The window opened
on a tangled growth
of shrub.
He moved his wooden desk.

Second reel, New Life:
a barbed-wire fence
rough cobblestones
a solitary tree
and brown leaves
falling, falling.

He moved the damn desk back.
O brave new world:
incipient jungle
just outside.

He drew the curtains
and stayed in.
But all day long
the mind projected
images

one tree alone
self-strangled shrub
and brown leaves
falling free

LECTURER

He came on like a navigator
with complicated options to unravel

who fifty minutes later
had not yet sorted out which way to travel.

FETE

Look that fellow how he staring
at the boys in the band
with a half-empty beer-bottle
dangling from he hand.

Hooked, man, gasping for air
and posing casual, he frown
then suck the beer
and rest the bottle down.

Room full of empties.

TEACHER

for Bill Carr

Your foreign intervention helped
identify our region. We
give thanks (now you have left us)
finally.

Remembering you, I celebrate
imprudent anger, I commemorate
your obstinate anxiety to share.
True men, you tried to teach us, show they care.

ON CAMPUS, MURDER

The gentlemen were rough
trade, and the world closed in
on you, grabbing, jabbing
in the eye, the belly of
your need. Kindness
was never enough.

Koo deh. Him dead fi true.
Sun-hot and the glare
of strangers
drilling through
pretences,
a swarm of judges
rubbishing
your delicate defences.

HAVING EYES THAT SEE

The blind man led by a little boy
goes tap-tap-tapping down the street,
and foolishly I feel accused
for having eyes that see.

That blind man at the bus stop regularly
feeling along the window's edge –
'Thanks, God bless you,' shuffling on –
breeds like a chigger in my mind.

And leafing through a magazine
I am confronted by an ad,
'Tell me, what colour is the wind?'

I shan't let spurious guilt
take hold and steer me
into gloom, and yet
I think I see
a shadowy connection.

MEETING

I

An unfamiliar bed
of radicals. And me
looking to root
out lies.

A nightmare –
comrade after comrade
springing
up to criticize!

I took
to planting
questions
in your eyes.

II

spuriously dry
we banter
knowing

something
critical
is growing
underground

a movement
threatening
solidarity

In the bookshop
and in his kitchen
he seemed the same
warm presence, quietly sharing
data, recommending things
to read, acknowledging
so much that others did not
deem progressive.

His instinct to include
attracted cultural allies
whose revolutionary impulses
they themselves disclaimed
at first, before they understood.

NURSERY

Everyone suddenly burst out screaming
and hurling plastic building-blocks;
the room was a riot of colour.

Did that autistic child have duller
things in mind, hugging his little box
of bricks and quietly beaming?

CASE HISTORY, JAMAICA

In 19-something X was born
in Jubilee Hospital, howling, black.

In 19- (any date plus four)
X went out to school.
They showed him pretty pictures
of his Queen.

When he was seven, in elementary school,
he asked what naygas were.
In secondary school he knew.
He asked in History one day
where slaves came from.
'Oh, Africa,' the master said.
'Get on with your work.'

Up at the university he didn't find himself;
and, months before he finally dropped out,
would ramble round the campus late at night
and daub his blackness on the walls.

BRIEF

Your dark eye is a prism
to reflect
the new world in its glass?

Shatter that rass
and roam
the darker continent
inside.

CABAL

Dem beg him, beg him, till dem sick
an tired – him wouldn sign him name
to what de most a dem waan lick
de opposition with. Him seh, 'Same

knife stick sheep stick goat,' an walk
out of de room. De big-man bus
a funny laugh. Nobody never talk
to him like dat. Him seh, 'Trust

me, eediot mus learn.' So, first of all,
we kick de eediot out de group. An den
we start de rumour seh him bawl
fi mercy when we check de books again –

yuh never know him tief? Yes, man, tief
like puss, unless yuh watchin him! An now
dat him expose, pure grief
to get another job. Him shoulda bow!

Me scratch your back, you scratch mine;
but if yuh tun traitor yuh must pay.
Dyamn fool! De eediot bwoy was tryin
to block de road. We move him out de way.

POLITICIAN NIGHTMARE

I'm in a meeting
sorting out

an everlasting list
of supplicants

and suddenly
I'm flying

low
above the city

and a mob
is reaching up

trying to drag me down

AFRO-SAXON

I

Another friend arraigns me:
too detached, he says,
absurdly free
of all the ways of feeling
true blacks, as a rule,
now share: Be funky, brother,
or be cool!

Okay. Though blackness isn't new
to me: ten, fifteen years ago
I didn't need
a uniform, my skin would do:
but I am learning, brother;
I'll succeed . . .

II

He never made it. Thought-
inspectors, quivering at the sight
of an Afro-Saxon on the road
towards the border, caught
him sneaking in-
to Blackness, radioed:
Don't let that nigger fool you, he is White!

THE HOUSE SLAVE

A drum thumps, faraway;
around the lamp my tribe of blood
are singing brothers home.

But soon that central fire will rage
too harsh for relics of the whip:
they'll burn this building,
fire these books, this art.

And these are my rooms now:
my pallid masters fled,
fleeing the only home I knew.
I'll stay another night,
sounding my tutored terror of the dark.

I AM THE MAN

I am the man that build his house on shit
I am the man that watch you bulldoze it
I am the man of no fixed address
Follow me now

I am the man that have no job
I am the man that have no vote
I am the man that have no voice
Hear me now

I am the man that have no name
I am the man that have no home
I am the man that have no hope
Nothing is mine

I am the man that file the knife
I am the man that make the bomb
I am the man that grab the gun
Study me now

FOR 1865

We hear you
bawling justice
justice
we want justice

echoing
a century
and a half
into the TV news

The killing time
has lingered
like a dump on fire
like the cries
of grieving

like the hegemonic
stench
of army
and police
destroying
in the name
of peace
and order

ADVISORY

They praise you for commitment,
your positive approach
to the whole heap o' problems
people broach.

Have fun being chatted-up,
but don't buy in-
to any sweet-mouth programme.
Do your own thing.

Remind them you're committed
to the line
that saying what you feel
is fine,

positive or negative
or in-between.
Don't let anybody
lock you in.

CATCH A NIGGER

At home with his creative curse
he lived inside; and (what was worse)
declined to share the public strain.
His beat was individual pain.

The censors grew more angry and more loud:
how dare he set himself outside the crowd?
'The times are critical. You're either for
or you're against us. This is war!'

And then a man with an enormous head
assaulted him. The victim bled
outside, in open view. Perhaps the pack
would sniff his blood and classify it black?

'Fee fi fo fum,
When you perform, our god is dumb;
Eeny meeny miney mo,
You're a Nigger Minstrel Show!'

He stanched the public wound, and bled
inside again. His blood was red.

FOR CONSCIOUSNESS

Ol' plantation wither,
factory close down,
brothers of de country
raisin' Cain in town.

An' now dem in de city
sweatin' blood dem fin'
is jus' like de same system
dem mean to lef' behin':

but agents of de owners-dem
is harder now to sight –
plenty busha doan ride horse
an' some doan t'ink dem white.

In de new plantation story
firs' t'ing dat have to know
is who an' who to tackle
when de call to battle blow.

TO AN EXPATRIATE FRIEND

Colour meant nothing. Anyone
who wanted help, had humour or was kind
was brother to you; categories of skin
were foreign; you were colour-blind.

And then the revolution. Black
and loud the horns of anger blew
against the long oppression; sufferers
cast off the precious values of the few.

New powers re-enslaved us all:
each person manacled in skin, in race.
You could not wear your paid-up dues;
the keen discriminators typed your face.

The future darkening, you thought it time
to say goodbye. It may be you were right.
It hurt to see you go; but, more,
it hurt to see you slowly going white.

When the battle started
he was quick to duck.
He lay on his face in the open street
cursing his luck.

'Come join us!' (voices from the left).
'Come help us in the fight!'
'Be honest with yourself; you're ours,'
said voices from the right.

Meanwhile the bullets overhead
were troubling him somewhat
and buildings burning either side
had made the middle hot.

He thought perhaps he'd better choose.
He crawled to join a side.
A bullet clapped him in the neck –
of course he died.

They left him face-down in the dust,
carcass going rotten.
Bullets whistled overhead.
He was forgotten.

A POET OF THE PEOPLE

The pressure of the public made it smart
to turn away from 'self-indulgent Art'.
He found immediate applause inviting,
and gave himself wholeheartedly to writing
poems for the people, loud and clear.

When people didn't seem to care
much whether he wrote well or not –
how was nothing, everything was what –
he changed his mind again. And so,
thinking to have another go
at 'self-indulgent Art', he turned
towards the woman he had spurned,
his ever-loving personal Muse,
believing she could not refuse
him. But she did. She left him there,
writing for the people, loud and clear.

NARCISSUS

They're lying; lying, all of them:
he never loved his shadow.
He saw it was another self
and tried to wring its neck.
Not love but murder on his mind,
he grappled with the other man
inside the lucid stream.

Only the surface broke.
Unblinking eyes
came swimming back in view.

At last he knew
he never would
destroy that other self.
And knowing made him shrink.

He shrank into a yellow-bellied flower.

OMENS

last night
a dream of feasting

today at noon
a green limb broken
in the wind

GREATEST SHOW ON EARTH

The Great Majumboes
(to the noise of drums)
feign danger every show:
vivid above the safety nets
they swing.

The Mighty Marvo cracks the whip:
well-drugged tigers lumber into line.

Between the tigers and the acrobats
I do my act I
sit on chairs that aren't there
I play for time
(between the tigers and the acrobats)
a dwarf
who owns no whip
and will not leave this ground.

BEHIND THE CURTAIN

Behind the curtain, when we knew
the audience hadn't come,
the ugly mood of histrionic sorrow
was broken by an actor playing dumb
patrician: 'Will the damn fools come tomorrow?'

resentfully awake
inside our bungalows

we hear
the cinematic roar of lions
in their cages

FABLE

The grey beast, smiling,
stretched a claw
to draw the artist in;
red with rage
the artist turned and spat.

'I cannot stand
the grey beast
with its coat and tie.
Leave me
to rear my roses
shape opinions
suffer books
paint pictures
love the people
choose true friends.'

The grey beast, placid, smiled.

The artist,
red with rage,
fired arrows
at the huge grey gut.

The grey beast, mocking, smiled.

And when the artist had the nerve
to turn and ask for help
the grey beast muttered sadly,
'You despise me. Help yourself.'

SOMETIMES

'Sometimes,' he said, 'when it was hot as hell
we'd go and capture scorpions for laughs,
and dig a trench around a little circle
in which we dumped the heap of them,
and pour in kerosene and light a fire.
Was fun to watch the devils fight,
and burn to death in trying to escape.
Scorpions are such beasts.'

MEETING THE MAGE

Charming, malicious, brilliant,
you posed your aching heart upon your sleeve
(yet so discreetly), breathing warm
to those who loved your sunshine humour,
passionate contempt, your well-turned
praises, witty mimicry –
oh, you were quite a boy, without conceit.

Yet, though so often self-deflating,
you held court all day long. I loved it.
While I was there I loved it; but,
free from that bright ambience,
irony took hold.

SATIRIST

Satirical vision:
bloodshot eyes
darting derision,
laughing at lies.

When the eyes turn in
will the dry mind grin?
If the eyes talk true
will the heart laugh too?

If the eyes don't lie
will the dry mind cry?
If the eyes go deep
will the cold heart weep?

DEATH AND THE MAIDEN

after Edvard Munch

Her partner is a skeleton.
Does the waltzing beauty know
that he will never let her go?
He'll have her when the dance is done.

He's put a bone between her legs.
Her fleshy body begs
for love, she holds him tight,
her gigolo, her slave tonight!

PRE-CARNIVAL PARTY

after Jules Romains

One evening in another town
– a little before Carnival –
a funny man with flies around
him crashed into a bar.

'Beauty-queen an' sagaboy,' he said,
'dey posin', but dey ain' fool me:
de one sure t'ing is all-yuh dead
dis time nex' century:

'yuh lookin' vague an' sad like when
yuh ain' know what to-duh.
Look alive! Before ah sen'
De side fo' yuh!'

Reminded of the loyal flies
buzzing round his face,
the people quickened into life –
jumped up and shook the place.

On what it was that made us jump,
injecting life into the fête,
the pundits waver or are dumb.
Was it the fear of flies or death?

A WORD

please to
burn the body
when i die
& scatter
ashes in the wind

so there is nothing
physical to focus on
when i am gone

& please to
let me linger
in the memory of a few
close friends & family
a month or two

A BIRTHDAY POEM

Peel-head john-crow circling

year after year habitually conveys
congratulations dead on time;

each year it wheezes, hovering:
'Happy birthday: you decline

hereafter, everything decays.'
Supernal mockery presents

that gliding messenger on time
each year, in pantomime

of blessing, wry malevolence
of joy before our wasting innocence.

HISTORIAN

for Elsa Goveia

& here we are
remembering
the dark

woman who
searched out meaning
in the dust

& left us
the enigma of her
going

JAMAICAN DANCE #2

for Oswald Russell

Bereavement singing
from the instrument,
interrogating death,
the nine-night
in your left hand
wringing grief.

Birds twittering
their fore-day call
and response.
Sammy dead-oh,
Sammy dead-oh.
Bawl, woman, bawl.

THE DAY MY FATHER DIED

The day my father died
I could not cry;
My mother cried,
Not I.

His face on the pillow
In the dim light
Wrote mourning to me,
Black and white.

We saw him struggle,
Stiffen, relax;
The face fell empty,
Dead as wax.

I'd read of death
But never seen.
My father's face, I swear,
Was not serene.

Topple that lie,
However appealing:
That face was absence
Of all feeling.

My mother's tears were my tears,
Each sob shook me:
The pain of death is living,
The dead are free.

For me my father's death
Was mother's sorrow;
That day was her day.
Loss was tomorrow.

YOUNG WIDOW, GRAVE

A wreath of mourners
at the grave. It gapes.
The people sing.
The service isn't meaning anything.

His secretary's legs look sleek in black.

The widow's looking farther back.
Across the gap, now flower-choked,
her swollen eyes have stumbled on
another man she lost; who poked
the fire, and when it stirred was gone.

That was another death.

FAREWELL FUNCTION

he basked in admiration
dreaming
paradise

until
his metamorphosis

into a morbid
out-of-body witness
at the operation

like a patient etherized
returning
from the edge

& catching an obituary
draught

GARDEN

after a shower
blackbirds preening on the grass
dressing for heaven

TERMINAL

She's withering
before our eyes

and no one
noticeably

cries
We do

the hopeful
ritual

each day
we bring

fresh fruit
we prattle

and we pray
for hours

Her room
is heavy

with the scent
of flowers

A CHANT AGAINST DEATH

for Aidan & Ruth

say family

          say friends

say wife

say love

    say life

say learning

         laughter

    sunlight

           rain

say cycle

        circle

music

   memory

say night & day

   say sun & moon

say

see you soon

POSTCARD

from Longarone

Green fields
a vineyard
red-roofed cottages
a farmer & his dog
before the flood

& here
at panel two
grey miles of waste
a desolating tract

What countervailing
message
do you scrawl
on this

this glossy *memento
mori*

MY RODNEY POEM

for Eddie Baugh
& in memory of Walter

I

He lived
a simple life

He was a man
who cared
when anybody hurt
not just the wretched
of the earth

He dared
to be involved
in nurturing
upheavals

II

Frustrated by
the host of evils
he seemed to me a good
man reaching for the moon

He died
too soon

EPITAPH

for Nita Barrow

Unusually perceptive human being,
genial, compassionate and wise,
she helped us see what she was seeing,
our true potential playing in her eyes.

SOPRANO

they say
she sang her heart out
day before she died

truth is
she sang her heart out
time after time

just like the day before
she soared
into another life

still singing
heaven

LYING IN STATE

Viewing the body endlessly
the people pass
tearfully relearning
that flesh is grass.

We're shuffling along
(the ritual declares)
to celebrate another life.
We mask our fears.

Peering at the face of death
the people pass
fearfully relearning:
All flesh is grass.

A DAUGHTER'S RECOLLECTION

My father smoked
and smoking killed him
in the end

but I'm remembering
that in my childhood
when he wiped my tears

the magic-making
handkerchief
smelt always
of tobacco

EXHIBITION

His early work was radiant
('resolutely sane', she said)
before the demons took him
to the shadow in his head.

Aficionados talk us through
the middle period, elegantly dread,
to what they call 'exhilarating darkness'
now he's dead.

AU REVOIR

He loved her madly,
cherishing her witty candour,
raunchy jokes,
tenacious *joie de vivre*.

After she left him for a nursing home,
each evening at their silent bungalow
the table would be set for two
and he would dine alone.

Last week Thursday, on his birthday,
after a whisky in the fading light,
he heard her breathe, 'Enough'.
He wiped his eyes and, like a courtier,
bowed low to kiss her shrivelled hand.

GRANNY

When Granny died
I stumbled in and out
her place, remembering
banana porridge, fumbling
her dog-eared bible,
faded bedspread,
musty cushions, hugging
memories of her love.

From the overflowing funeral
this fingled programme
is a talisman I carry
everywhere. Love is with me still.

DINNER PARTY

Between convivial
flashes of hilarity
a brooding presence.

Half his friends have died,
and each white bird
is like a premonition.

He shuffles towards
the car door, struggles in
and waves goodbye.

DIPTYCH

I

when the wild guitarist
making too much noise
was thrown out by
his wutliss friend
he hanged himself

the day the music stopped
i came by
& was blasted
by the poui tree's
golden indifference

II

when the drunken painter
messing up the place
was thrown out by
the woman paying the rent
he hanged himself

& when he died
she gave away his last
pathetic canvasses
of sombre figures
& the poui weeping gold

LEGION

I

in the agonising
calm

a self-
destructive dread

erupted
from the boneyard

howling

II

deadly bastard
fucking up
our lives

an intimate
disaster

littering the tombstones
with his shredded poems

III

dark dark dark
inside
the world i want
to bury

yerri mi mi nana
yerri mi . . .

CHECKING OUT

I slam the door. 'Dear, are you positive
there's nothing left?' Well, no:
something remains, I'm sure of that:

some vestige of our lives in this bare flat
will linger, some impulse will outlive
our going, recycled in the flow

of being. We never leave,
we always have to go.

Acknowledgements

Some of these poems have appeared in the following journals and newspapers: *Aqueduct*, *Ariel*, *Arts Review*, *Atlanta Review*, *Bim*, *Callaloo*, *Caribbean Quarterly*, *The Caribbean Writer*, *Cincinnati Poetry Review*, *English*, *Graham House Review*, *Greenfield Review*, *The Independent*, *International Portland Review*, *Interviewing the Caribbean*, *The Jamaica Daily News*, *The Jamaica Gleaner*, *Jamaica Journal*, *The Jamaica Sunday Observer*, *Kyk-Over-Al*, *The Literary Half-Yearly*, *Mississippi Review*, *Nimrod*, *Now*, *Obsidian III*, *Outposts*, *Pathways*, *Pepperpot*, *Planet*, *Poetry International*, *Poetry Wales*, *Poui*, *Public Opinion*, *Race Today*, *Savacou*, *Tapia*, *The Times Literary Supplement*, *Trinidad and Tobago Review*, *Wasafiri* and *World Literature Today*.

INDEX OF TITLES

INDEX OF FIRST LINES